SING ME A STORY

Sing a song of six - pence, a pock - et full of rye,

JANE BROWNE

Crown Publishers, Inc.
New York

To Barbara and the playgroup

Published in 1991 in the United States of America by Crown Publishers, Inc., a
Random House company, 225 Park Avenue South, New York, New York 10003.
Originally published in Great Britain in 1991 by Julia MacRae Books.
CROWN is a trademark of Crown Publishers, Inc.
Manufactured in Hong Kong
Library of Congress Cataloging-in-Publication Data
Browne, Jane. Sing me a story: action songs to sing and play/Jane Browne. 1 score.
Summary: Features thirteen songs based on well-known nursery rhymes and fairy
tales. Instructions for making action movements accompany each song. 1. Children's
songs. 2. Games with music. 3. Nursery rhymes, English — Musical settings.
4. Fairy tales — Musical settings. [1. Songs. 2. Games with music.
3. Nursery rhymes. 4. Fairy tales.] I. Title.
M1993.B87S5   1991   90-753578

ISBN 0-517-58353-4

10 9 8 7 6 5 4 3 2 1

First American Edition

INTRODUCTION

Twelve years ago, when I finished my classical training as a violinist, I began teaching the violin, viola, and piano and working as a freelance performer. My interest in preschool music was then aroused by the birth of my two children, and I formed a preschool music group at my home. Finding very little suitable material available for this age group, I began to write and compose my own songs.

Sing Me A Story is a compilation drawn from the material I have written and arranged, based on familiar nursery rhymes and fairy tales. The combination of music, words, and suggested actions adds to the enjoyment of learning the song. Most preschool music books have, on the whole, been designed primarily for the use of teachers. I hope this book can be used as a practical songbook in playgroups and schools, and that it can also be shared and enjoyed by children and their parents at home.

— Jane Browne

Ellen　　Kelly　　Michael　　Joanna　　Richard　　Joseph　　Victoria　　Chi Man　　Megan

SING A SONG OF SIXPENCE

Sing a song of six - pence, a pock - et full of rye,

four and twen - ty black - birds baked in a pie.   When the pie was o - pened, the

birds be-gan to sing, Oh, was-n't that a dain-ty dish to set be-fore the king?

The king was in his counting house
Counting out his money.

The queen was in the parlor
Eating bread and honey.

The maid was in the garden
Hanging out the clothes,

When down came a blackbird
And pecked off her nose.

OWL

There's a wide-eyed owl with a poin-ted nose, two poin-ted ears, and claws for its toes. It

sits in a tree and looks at you, flaps its wings and says twit t -woo-oo!

LITTLE MISS MUFFET

HUMPTY DUMPTY

Hump - ty Dump - ty sat on the wall. Hump - ty Dump - ty had a great fall.

All the king's hors-es and all the king's men could-n't put Hump-ty to - geth-er a-gain.

HICKORY DICKORY DOCK

Hick-o - ry dick-o - ry dock,_____ the mouse ran up_ the clock._____ The

clock struck one, DONG, the mouse ran down, Hick-o - ry dick-o - ry dock._____

OLD KING COLE

Old King Cole was a mer-ry old soul and a mer-ry old soul was he.   He called for his pipe and he

called for his bowl and he called for his fid-dl-ers three.   Now ev-ery fid-dl-er   he had a fid-dle and a

ve-ry fine fid-dle had he.   Yo-ho-ho cried old King Cole, and the fid-dlers played fid-dle dee

dee.   There's none so rare as   can com-pare with King Cole and his fid-dl-ers   three.

THE GRAND OLD DUKE OF YORK

The Grand Old Duke of York, he had ten thou - sand men. He

marched them up to the top of the hill and he marched them down a - gain. And

G   Am   D7

when they were up they were up, and when they were down they were down, and

G   C   D D7 G

when they were on - ly half - way up, they were nei - ther up nor down.

Old Woman

There was an old wo-man tossed up in a bas - ket nine-ty-nine times as high as the moon.

Where she was go-ing I could not but ask it, for in her hand she car-ried a broom. Old

wo-man, old wo-man, old wo-man, quoth I, Where are you go-ing to, up__ so high? To

sweep the cob-webs from the sky.___ Will you come with me? Aye, by and by.___

HERE WE GO ROUND THE MULBERRY BUSH

Chorus

Here we go round the mul - berry bush, the mul - berry bush, the mul - berry bush.

Here we go round the mul - berry bush so ___ ear - ly in ___ the morn - ing.

Verse 1
This is the way we wash our face,
Wash our face, wash our face,
This is the way we wash our face
So early in the morning.
Chorus

Verse 2
This is the way we brush our hair . . . etc.
Chorus

Verse 3
This is the way we clean our teeth . . . etc.
Chorus

Verse 4
This is the way we put on our clothes . . . etc.
Chorus

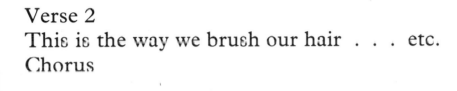

Verse 5
This is the way we walk to school . . . etc.
Chorus

JACK AND THE BEANSTALK

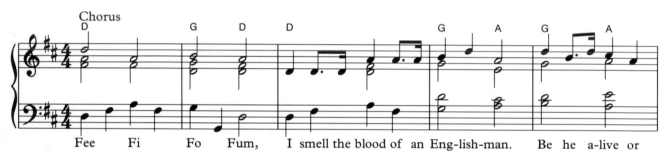

Fee   Fi   Fo   Fum,   I smell the blood of an Eng-lish-man.   Be   he   a-live   or

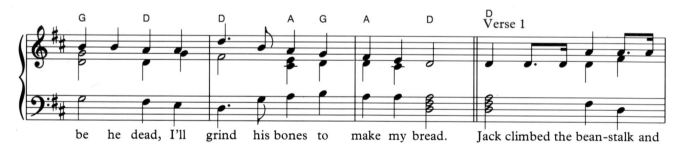

be   he dead, I'll   grind   his bones   to   make my bread.   Jack climbed the bean-stalk and

what did he see? A great big gi-ant want-ing Jack for his tea. MIGH-TY CRASH!

Verse 2
Jack stole the magic hen and ran away.
But he climbed back up again another day . . .
Chorus

Verse 3
Jack stole the magic harp and climbed to the floor.
The giant climbed behind with a terrible ROAR! . . .
Chorus

Verse 4
Jack took up his ax with a chop and a bash.
The giant fell down with a mighty CRASH!

GOLDILOCKS AND THE THREE BEARS

When Gold - i-locks went to the house of the bears, Oh, what did her blue eyes

see?_____ A bowl that was huge, a bowl that was small, and a bowl that was

tin-y, and that was all. And she count-ed them, one – two – three._____

Verse 2
When Goldilocks went to the house of the bears,
Oh, what did her blue eyes see?
A chair that was huge, a chair that was small,
And a chair that was tiny, and that was all.
And she counted them, one – two – three.

Verse 3
When Goldilocks went to the house of the bears,
Oh, what did her blue eyes see?
A bed that was huge, a bed that was small,
And a bed that was tiny, and that was all.
And she counted them, one – two – three.

Verse 4
When Goldilocks went to the house of the bears,
Oh, what did her blue eyes see?
A bear that was huge, a bear that was small,
And a bear that was tiny, and that was all.
And they growled at her roar – roar – ROAR!

SLEEPING BEAUTY

There was a prin-cess long a-go, long a-go, long a-go. There was a prin-cess long a-go, long a-go.

Verse 2
And she lived in a big high tower,
Big high tower, big high tower.
And she lived in a big high tower,
Long ago.

Verse 3
One day a bad queen cast a spell,
Cast a spell, cast a spell.
One day a bad queen cast a spell,
Long ago.

Verse 4

The princess slept for a hundred years,
Hundred years, hundred years.
The princess slept for a hundred years,
Long ago.

Verse 5

A great big forest grew around,
Grew around, grew around.
A great big forest grew around,
Long ago.

Verse 6

A gallant prince came riding by,
Riding by, riding by.
A gallant prince came riding by,
Long ago.

Verse 7

He chopped the trees down with his sword,
With his sword, with his sword.
He chopped the trees down with his sword,
Long ago.

Verse 8

He kissed her hand to wake her up,
Wake her up, wake her up.
He kissed her hand to wake her up,
Long ago.

Verse 9

So everybody's happy now,
Happy now, happy now.
So everybody's happy now,
Happy now.

SNOW WHITE

Chorus

Mir - ror___ mir - ror   on   the   wall,   who   is   the   fair - est   of   them   all?

You,   oh_   Queen,   have   beau - ty___   rare,   but   Snow White   is   ten   times more   fair.

Verse 1
Seven little men who lived in a wood,
Tried to save Snow White as hard as they could.
When the wicked queen gave an apple to Snow White,
From the poisoned half she took a bite.

Chorus . . .

Verse 2
A handsome prince found Snow White sleeping,
Seven little men around her weeping.
He gave her a kiss and she woke with laughter.
They married and then lived happily ever after.

| Ellen | Kelly | Michael | Joanna | Richard | Joseph | Victoria | Chi Man | Megan |

RAYMOND ARROYO

New York Times bestselling author

THE UNEXPECTED LIGHT OF
THOMAS ALVA EDISON

Illustrated by

KRISTINA GEHRMANN

ZONDER**kidz**

To all the mothers—like Rebecca and Lynda—who see
the promise in their children long before the world does.

—RA

ZONDERKIDZ

The Unexpected Light of Thomas Alva Edison
Copyright © 2023 by Raymond Arroyo
Illustrations © 2023 by Raymond Arroyo

Requests for information should be addressed to:

Zonderkidz, 3900 *Sparks Drive, Grand Rapids, Michigan* 49546

Hardcover ISBN 978-0-310-79923-8
Ebook ISBN 978-0-310-79924-5

Library of Congress Cataloging-in-Publication Data
Names: Arroyo, Raymond, author. | Gehrmann, Kristina, illustrator.
Title: The unexpected light of Thomas Alva Edison / by Raymond Arroyo.
Description: Grand Rapids : Zonderkidz, [2023] | Audience: Ages 4-8 |
   Summary: "From New York Times bestselling author and news anchor Raymond
   Arroyo comes a picture book biography of one of America's most famous
   inventors, Thomas Alva Edison, and a story about how a small spark can
   create a big light. No one thought much of young Thomas Alva Edison. He
   couldn't focus at school and caused trouble around the house. But where
   others saw a distracted and mischievous boy, his mother saw imagination
   and curiosity. When he was only seven years old, Al, as he was called as
   a young child, got kicked out of school and from then on his mother
   oversaw his rigorous at-home education while also allowing him great
   freedom to explore and dream. Those early years of encouragement and
   loving guidance formed the man who would apply those valuable lessons as
   well as his rich imagination to inventing the phonograph, the motion
   picture camera, the light bulb and more. Inside, readers will: meet the
   larger-than-life personality of Thomas Alva Edison, hear a tale of an
   underdog overcoming all the odds, learn about the power of curiosity,
   and take a carefully researched and actively told romp through
   history"-- Provided by publisher.
Identifiers: LCCN 2022005560 (print) | LCCN 2022005561 (ebook) | ISBN
   9780310799238 (hardcover) | ISBN 9780310799245 (ebook)
Subjects: LCSH: Edison, Thomas A. (Thomas Alva), 1847-1931--Juvenile
   literature. | Edison, Thomas A. (Thomas Alva), 1847-1931--Childhood and
   youth--Juvenile literature. | Inventors--United States--Juvenile
   literature. | Mothers and sons--Juvenile literature.
Classification: LCC TK140.E3 A77 2023 (print) | LCC TK140.E3 (ebook) |
   DDC 621.3092 [B]--dc23/eng/20220909
LC record available at https://lccn.loc.gov/2022005560
LC ebook record available at https://lccn.loc.gov/2022005561

Illustrations: Kristina Gehrmann
Editor: Katherine Jacobs
Design and art direction: Cindy Davis

Printed in Italy

As a baby, little Al Edison slept in a dark,
windowless attic. But there was light within him.

3

Al was forever getting into trouble, which sometimes happens when you're curious.

He was interested in everything from how birds flew to where bees lived to how steamboats moved along the big canals behind his house.

Whenever his mother wasn't watching, he snuck down to the waterway for a closer look.

Sometimes he got a bit too close!

But most of all, Al wanted to know how things worked.
He explored the town, noticing everything, and he sketched
whatever drew his attention, like the shop signs in the town square.

Once, when he wondered how a grain elevator carried grain up into its storage bins, he climbed inside, and found out for himself.

At home, Al peppered his parents with questions: "Who?" "What?"
"Why?" "How?"

After a while his father had enough.

"I don't know!" he yelled.

"Why don't you know?" Al asked.

His mother patiently answered his questions.

8

When Al asked, "Why does the goose squat on the eggs?" she said,
"To keep them warm."

"Why does she keep them warm?"

"To hatch them, my dear."

Al's eyes widened. "Keeping the eggs warm makes the little geese come out?"

"Yes."

Al had an idea.

9

His father found him hours later in a neighbor's barn, lying on top of a big nest filled with goose and chicken eggs. This might have been Thomas Alva Edison's first experiment. He didn't hatch any geese, but he did manage to outrage his father.

Later, when Al was six years old, his curiosity about fire got the best of him. He set a small blaze in his father's barn "just to see what it would do."

The blaze torched the entire building and the flames nearly spread across town. His furious dad punished him in the public square. As painful as it was, it did nothing to stifle Al's curiosity.

Against his father's wishes, Al would sometimes run along the canal to the workshop of a man called "the Mad Miller of Milan." Sam Winchester, a flour mill owner, was trying to create a balloon big enough to carry people into the sky. He even burned down his own mill during one of the experiments—which fascinated Al.

He would press his face against the workshop window as the miller tinkered and fiddled with the hydrogen needed to lift his balloon. If one approach didn't work, the miller would try something else. The intensity of those experiments showed young Al that hands-on hard work could unlock amazing discoveries.

When he was seven years old, Al's family moved to Port Huron, Michigan. There, he was enrolled in Reverend G.B. Engle's one-room schoolhouse. Gone were the trips to the canal and the daring, hands-on experiments. During the boring lectures, Al fidgeted, daydreamed, and didn't respond to questions at all.

He's "addled," the schoolmaster announced publicly, convinced that Al Edison couldn't be taught. A heartbroken Al ran home to his mother in tears.

The next day, Mrs. Edison stormed into the school with her son in tow. She told
Reverend Engle that he "didn't know what he was talking about." She had seen
the light in her son and knew he "had more brains than" even the teacher himself.
From that day on, she told the schoolmaster, she would educate Al at home.

Mrs. Edison introduced Al to Shakespeare and Charles Dickens. He read *A School Compendium of Natural and Experimental Philosophy*, from cover to cover. The book explained electricity, mechanics, and the electric telegraph.

Al was so intrigued that he sketched and then built his own telegraph line to a neighbor's house.

Chemistry books inspired ten-year-old Al to build a lab at home.
To protect her furniture, his mother relocated it to the family cellar.

Downstairs, his attempts to create a battery with jars of
acid caused the occasional explosion.

"He will blow us all up," his father fumed.

"Let him be," his mother said. "Al knows what he's about."

Money was always tight for the Edisons. So at twelve years old, Al convinced his parents to allow him to sell newspapers, candy, and food aboard the new Grand Trunk Railway, a train line that ran between Port Huron and Detroit.

The clatter and squeal of the train barely phased Al. This was when he began to realize he had lost most of his hearing.

But deafness proved a gift for young Edison. "In my isolation, I had time to think things out," he later said. "Deafness probably drove me to reading." During the six and half hour layover in Detroit each day, Al could be found at the public library. He began with the books on the lowest shelves of the library, and read his way to the top shelves in no time.

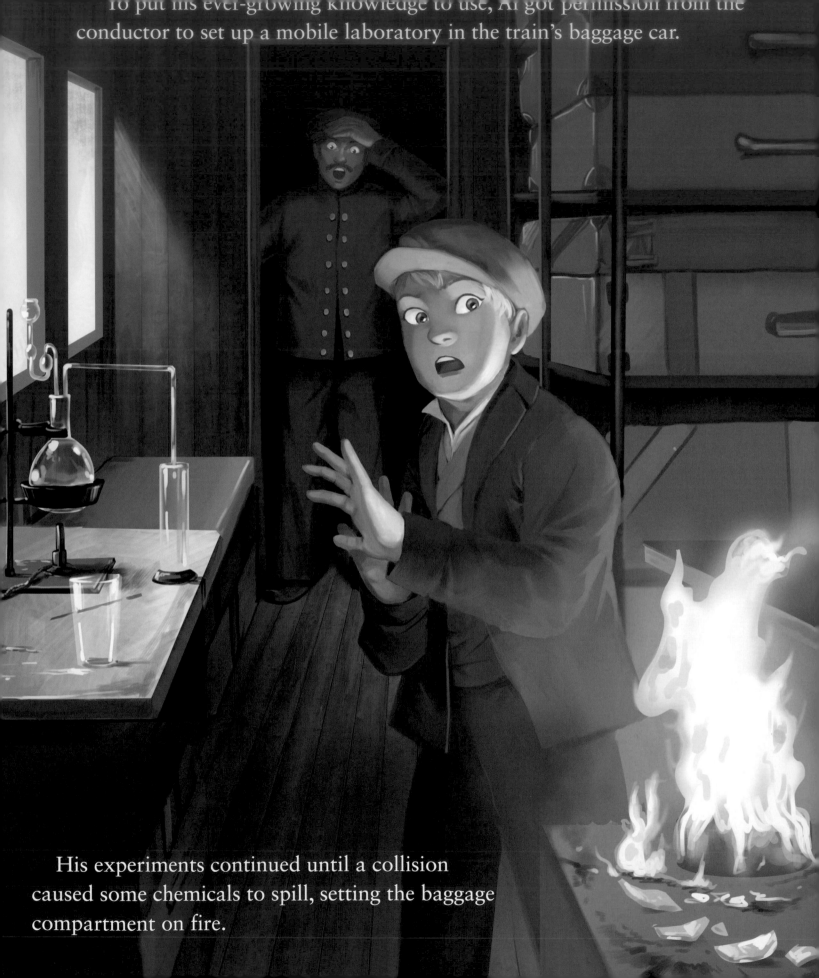

His experiments continued until a collision caused some chemicals to spill, setting the baggage compartment on fire.

Unstoppable, Al used recycled metal type and an old handpress to print his own newspaper in the train's baggage car. The *Weekly Herald* was filled with death notices, local stories, and gossip. The paper lasted until a man, upset by something Al had printed, threw him into the St. Clair River.

One afternoon, at the Mount Clemens station, Al was selling papers on the platform while his train changed cars. Suddenly a boxcar broke free and rolled toward a three year old child playing on the tracks. Al dropped his papers, leapt off the platform, and scooped up the child, saving his life.

The child's father, James Mckenzie, was the station telegrapher. To thank Al for saving his son, Mckenzie offered to teach Edison how to use the telegraph.

Al remembered the homemade telegraph line he had strung to his neighbor's house and imagined himself tapping out dashes and dots on a real machine, sending messages for much longer distances. He accepted the offer.

By the time he was sixteen years old, Al dropped his nickname and began using his first name, Tom. He was now a real plug telegrapher. But tapping a metal key to send messages across the country wasn't enough to satisfy Tom's curiosity.

He had ideas about how the power of electricity could improve daily life. So he created his first invention: an automatic voting machine. He tried to sell it to congress, but they weren't interested.

Then came a blow Tom never expected: He received a telegram that his mother had died. He rushed home for the funeral of the first person who believed in him—the one who kindled the light of his curiosity.

To honor his mother, and to prove himself worthy of her confidence, he threw himself into his work. In 1876, Tom opened what he called "the invention factory" in Menlo Park, New Jersey. Here, he and his "muckers" —a team of curious inventors and experimenters—turned dreams into reality.

Chock-full of inventions and inspirations, Tom would experiment through the night, taking short naps on the lab's workbenches. He threw himself over tables, furiously scrawling ideas in his notebooks.

What kind of device could record sound?

How would one capture moving images?

Which material could conduct enough electricity to extend the glow of a light bulb?

The current of ingenuity surged through him.

And inventions flowed out of Tom.

Thomas Alva Edison filled more than 3,000 notebooks with design sketches. He created the light bulb, the phonograph to record music, the motion picture camera, and so much more.

Springing from those jars of acid he mixed in his mother's basement so many years earlier, he invented the alkaline storage battery. But the light of invention within Tom might never have illuminated the world, had it not been for a mother who first saw the glow of curiosity in her Al.

Author's Note

It was Edison's comment late in life about his mother that drew me to his story and became the heart of this Turnabout Tale. The great inventor said: "My mother was the making of me … I did not have my mother for very long but in that length of time she cast over me an influence which has lasted all my life. The good effects of her early training I can never lose. If it had not been for her appreciation and her faith in me at a critical time in my experience, I should very likely never had become an inventor."

We often forget that talent is nurtured and revealed by love and belief. Nancy Edison, a former schoolteacher in Canada, understood the inherent spark in her boy and his unique gifts. She was tough on him, making him study while the other boys played. Edison said his mother taught him how to "read good books quickly and correctly." She is perhaps the most important and overlooked aspect of the Edison story.

Not only did his mother give him the confidence to pursue his passions and gather knowledge, but both his parents were hard workers. Thomas Edison carried that work ethic into adulthood. Forsaking sleep, meals, and time off, he practically lived in his lab. His was a process of excited, hands-on experimentation, marked by much trial and error. Edison's childlike curiosity never dimmed. There are stories of him hurling himself over worktables to see experiments close up and madly recording his observations in notebooks. The great inventor would often, by his own admission, pick up where the last inventor left off. He was a lifelong problem solver who pushed for solutions where others had given up. During his 84 years, Edison secured 1,093 patents, not only lighting up cities but revolutionizing the lives of people around the world. Edison's inventions from the phonograph to the first electric car not only enlightened his age, but our own. "Every wrong attempt discarded is another step forward," he said. "Sticking to it is the genius."

That approach applies not only to inventions, but to people as well. As Nancy Edison attests: The genius is sometimes found by sticking to them—and by them.

Further Reading and Bibliography

Adkins, Jan, *Thomas Edison*; New York, DK Publishing, 2009.

Baldwin, Neil, *Edison Inventing the Century*; New York, Hyperion, 1995.

Delano, Marfe' Ferguson; *Inventing the Future, The Photography of Thomas Alva Edison*; Washington, DC, National Geographic, 2002.

Josephson, Matthew, *Edison*; New York, McGraw-Hill, 1959.

Rutgers University Thomas Edison Papers Collection: edison.rutgers.edu/